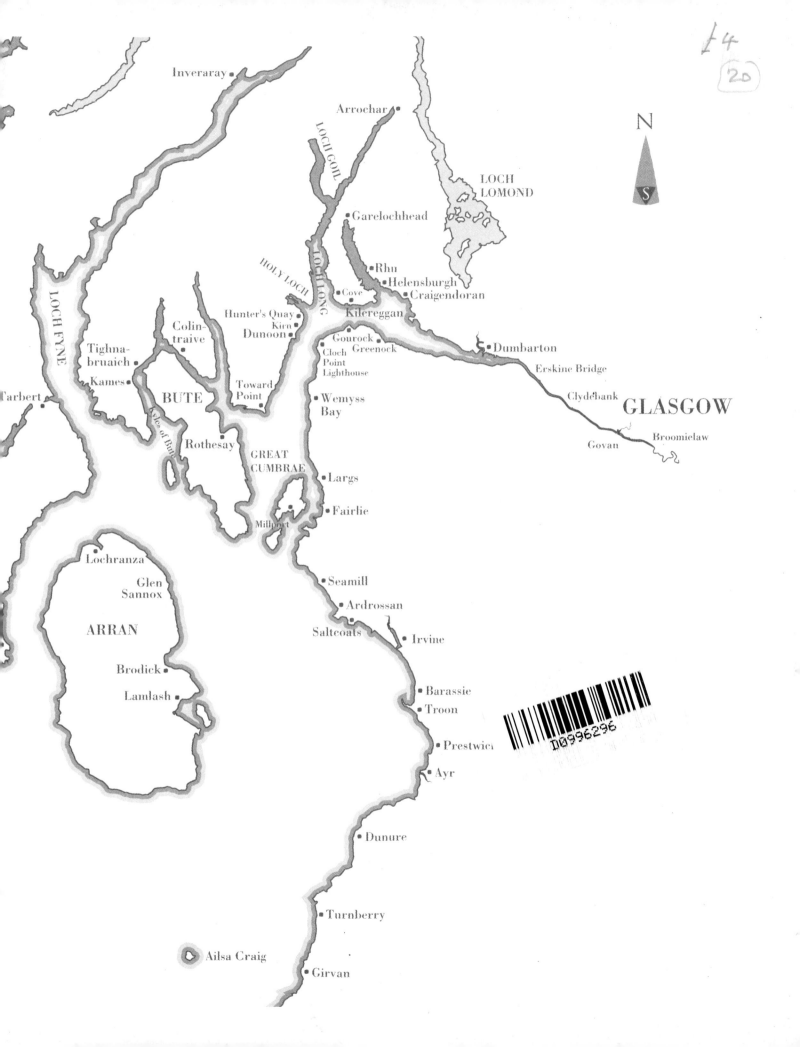

DOON THE WATTER

THE HERALD
BOOK OF THE CLYDE
VOLUME 2

Doon the WATTER

A CENTURY OF HOLIDAYS ON THE CLYDE

ROBERT JEFFREY & IAN WATSON

First published 1999
by Black & White Publishing Ltd, Edinburgh
A B&W Publishing imprint
ISBN 1 902927 04 4
Copyright © Scottish Media Newspapers
Introduction copyright © Robert Jeffrey & Ian Watson

British Library Cataloguing in Publication Data:
A catalogue record for this book is available
from the British Library.

Copies of many of the photographs in this book
are available for personal or commercial use.
Contact: Photo Sales Department,
Scottish Media Newspapers,
195 Albion Street, Glasgow, G1 1QP,
quoting the reference number shown in
brackets after the caption.

Printed by Bookprint

CONTENTS

ACKNOWLEDGEMENTS

This book is a tribute to the skill and dedication of
The Herald and *Evening Times* staff photographers
down the years, whose work has produced
one of the world's great picture archives.

The assistance of the following people in the
preparation of this book is gratefully acknowledged:
Suzanne Harris, Fiona Weir, Alistair Nicol, Tom Noble,
Cameron Melville, John Davidson, Gordon Irving, Bill Niven,
Jane McKay and the staff of The Herald and Evening Times
Picture Library—Malcolm Beaton, Jim McNeish,
Tony Murray, Ben Adams, Catherine Turner,
Lisa Turner and Grace Gough.
Photographs on pages 3 & 5 by
kind permission of the Annan Gallery.

INTRODUCTION

The family album is a potent symbol of past and present. There is barely a house in the land without a drawerful of fading photographs. Untouched for months, or years on end, the photo albums are opened on a whim and the memories come flooding back.

The remarkable photographic archives of the *Herald, Evening Times* and *Sunday Herald* contain around seven million pictures. The collection, one of the largest in Europe, is to some extent Scotland's family album. Great liners taking to the sea, dignitaries visiting Glasgow or moments of political significance like the raising of the red flag in George Square are all there. It also has rather more than a drawerful of photographs which capture the lighter side of Scottish life!

The trades', or Fair, holidays in July saw a mass exodus from Glasgow and the surrounding towns down to the Clyde coast. Likewise at the spring and autumn holiday weekends. The major resorts—Rothesay, Dunoon, Largs, Troon, Ayr and Prestwick—bulged under the huge influx of holidaymakers from April until September. In these halcyon days fleets of steamers criss-crossed the Firth of Clyde.

But the story of the Firth is not just about holidays. It is often overlooked now, but at the end of the 19th century the boat was the principal means of communication between the towns dotted around the fjords and islands of the Clyde estuary. Places like Campbeltown at the southern end of the Kintyre peninsula were difficult to reach by road. Even Inveraray, now a mere 90 minutes by car from Glasgow, was an arduous land journey.

Hundreds of vessels ploughed up and down and to and fro across the Firth in all weathers, carving names like Kilcreggan, Innellan, Kirn, Dunoon and Wemyss Bay deep into the memories of Clydesiders. The combination of rail and steamer opened up the beautiful Cowal and Kintyre peninsulas and the islands of Bute, Cumbrae and Arran. The city dwellers flocked in their thousands for a couple of weeks in the fresh air away from oppressive living conditions and the grind and grime of shipyard, mine or steelworks. And many an infirm child, lungs damaged by TB, would be sent from the city for anything up to six months to a local authority-run home on the bracing coast.

All this brought the phrase "Doon the Watter" into the West of Scotland vocabulary.

Apart from journeys to far-away Campbeltown or the Western Isles you could take the train to Gourock, Wemyss Bay, Craigendoran or Ardrossan and from there sail to any number of resorts. Everyone had a favourite, perhaps Millport with its bike rides, golf and sailing, or maybe the more boisterous Rothesay or Dunoon. Ayr (and nearby Butlins), Girvan, Troon and Prestwick had their devotees who returned year after year. Often a "wee house down the coast" was bought and handed down from generation to generation.

For the holidaymaker the beach might have been the main attraction but in the evenings, or on a rain-sodden afternoon, there were always the "pictures" or variety shows in the Ayr Gaiety, Barrfields Pavilion in Largs, Rothesay Winter Gardens or the Cosy Corner in Dunoon. Many big stars started their careers entertaining at the seaside . . . Jack Anthony, Donald Peers, Robert Wilson, Chick Murray and Maidie, and Pat Kirkwood among others. In the twenties the legendary performers Harry Lauder and Will Fyffe played the Clyde seaside theatres.

Ayr races were a huge attraction with vast crowds watching the Gold Cup—cheering on thrilling victories by the likes of Roman Warrior or Able Albert. Prestwick had its air show, swimming galas attracted thousands and golfers enjoyed the classic links courses, Turnberry, Troon, Prestwick and Western Gailes. Those who didn't play flocked to watch much-loved stars like Palmer, Nicklaus and Player face the challenge of Scottish courses whose names are legendary the world over.

But times change. Today the *Waverley* is the only surviving link to the great pleasure steamers of the past. Ferries still run from Gourock, Wemyss Bay and Ardrossan, but these utilitarian vessels don't have the magic of their predecessors . . . *Lord of the Isles, Jeanie Deans, Lucy Ashton*, the *Duchess of Montrose* and *Duchess of Hamilton* and many more.

The photographs in this book recall the pleasures of simpler times—before a holiday meant a taxi to Glasgow airport, a tour of the duty free shop, a few drinks on the plane and then a bus journey to some high-rise hotel on the dusty shores of the Mediterranean.

The pleasure of a sunset stroll on the prom with a vinegar-soaked fish supper wrapped in newspaper. A needle match on the putting green with the kids. A coffee or speciality ice-cream in one of the many Italian cafes. All hugely enjoyed.

A trip round the bay for a shilling, a bus tour up to the Argyll hills—these were the attractions and these are the photographs that bring back to life the days when people travelled to the seaside resorts by train, rickety bus or steamer. On the steamers they danced, impromptu, to the ship's band, had a sing-song in the bar or simply gazed in awe as some of the finest scenery in the world slipped by.

As a new millennium dawns, the beauty of the Firth of Clyde is still a magnet for tourists. Its leisure facilities, world class golf, yachting, hill-walking and hospitality will always captivate the visitor. These pictures, culled from Scotland's family album, not only bring back memories—they celebrate the enduring delights of a trip Doon the Watter.

RJ & IW

BROOMIELAW TO HELENSBURGH & GOUROCK

The Broomielaw was the legendary starting point for journeys Doon the Watter. This evocative 1874 photograph captures the era when steam began to take over from sail. The north bank of the Clyde is packed with pleasure steamers while on the south side there is a forest of sailing ship masts. The Broomielaw waiting room advertises refreshments for the crowds who thronged this busy city centre departure point. *(DW001)*

This is the wharf at Broomielaw as it was around 1880. At one stage more than 30 ships were needed to cater for trippers leaving Glasgow for days out or extended holidays at the coastal resorts. Even after the Second World War, boats left from the heart of Glasgow for the dozens of piers at towns large and small down the Firth. *(DW002)*

Right: The *Iona*, the *Benmore* and the *Daniel Adamson* prepare for a journey down to the Tail of the Bank and beyond in 1895. The various cargo boats tied up are a reminder of the days when Glasgow's river was a vital artery for commerce. *(DW003)*

Five steamers at the Broomielaw in 1914. Passengers for the outside steamers embarked across the inner ships. The original caption tells us that the vessels on view are the *Lady Rowena*, the *Isle of Cumbrae, Isle of Skye, Ivanhoe* and the *Isle of Arran*. *(DW004)*

Right: The tradition of firms having nights out or away days Doon the Watter carried right on into the 1990s, notably on the ever popular PS *Waverley*. This is the staff of the famous Glasgow furniture store Bows of High Street setting off in 1933 on a Diamond Jubilee sail through the Kyles of Bute to Tighnabruaich. The good humour brought on by such trips—often involving significant intake of refreshments—is evident! *(DW005)*

DECK CHAIRS
CAN BE
HAD
ON BOARD
AT 6d EACH
PER DAY.

The *King Edward* leaving Broomielaw packed with happy holidaymakers. Deckchairs, if you could find a place to put one, were sixpence a day. *(DW006)*

Queen Mary II slides away from the riverbank to head down to the Kyles on an outing in 1958. This famous Clyde pleasure steamer had at this stage in her life only one funnel, having originally had two. The change had come a year earlier when she was converted to oil burning by Denny's of Dumbarton. *(DW007)*

Above: Six hundred trippers aged 70 and over, from Paisley, were the guests of Paisley town council on this *Queen Mary II* trip in the early 1950s, when the famous steamer sported two funnels. Again, the destination was the Kyles of Bute. *(DW008)*

Right: Another scene from the 1950s: the *Duchess of Montrose* passes a dredger, while on the north bank the *Royal Scotsman*, a famous name on the long defunct Glasgow-Belfast run, lies awaiting passengers. There's not an inch to spare on the packed pleasure steamer. *(DW009)*

Left: The *Waverley*, the much-loved last sea-going paddle-steamer in the world, has become something of an icon on the Clyde. This striking shot taken from the Erskine Bridge shows her classic lines. *(DW010)*

Above: A surprising number of people enjoyed their trips Doon the Watter in the unromantic surroundings of the sludge boat. Here the *Garroch Head* is photographed from almost the same position on the Erskine Bridge as the *Waverley* in the previous shot. This is a particularly poignant photograph as the vessel was making its final journey down the Clyde in December 1998 before being taken out of service because of new regulations prohibiting the dumping of sewage. From around the turn of the century Glasgow sewage had been processed at Shieldhall and Dalmuir. The residue after the processing, known as sludge, was taken downriver and dumped off Garroch Head on the south-east corner of Bute. A tradition grew up allowing passengers to make the journey from Glasgow to the dumping grounds and back. A great free day out on scrupulously clean boats, for pensioners and charity groups as well as councillors and their friends! *(DW011)*

Above: The bus was a popular method of reaching the Clyde resorts. This is Glasgow's West Nile Street, an important departure point in the 1930s. The battered suitcases and flat caps are evocative of the period. *(DW012)*

Left: North Drive behind the now-demolished St Enoch railway station was also an embarkation point for trips to the coast. This bus is preparing to leave on the Gourock via Renfrew run. The station and attached hotel were demolished in the 1970s and eventually replaced by one of the city's landmarks—the gigantic "glass house" that is the eye-catching St Enoch Centre, a typical late 20th century attraction for anyone looking for a little retail refreshment. *(DW013)*

Central Station in August 1937. The manual destination boards were a famous feature of the station until they were superseded by a huge electronic information board. *(DW014)*

The modern convenience of a luggage trolley was not available in the railway stations in 1915. This would appear to be a well-heeled group. The husband might have been kitted out from the famous Glasgow outfitter R W Forsyth whose shop is just visible in the background. *(DW015)*

Cycling was always popular with holidaymakers Doon the Watter, especially at Millport on the Isle of Cumbrae where hiring bikes to take you round the island remains popular to this day. But you could take your two wheels on holiday with you as this 1919 photograph shows. The schoolgirls were catching a train at St Enoch. No problems with getting bikes into the guard's van in those days! *(DW016)*

Outside St Enoch in the 1950s. Happy faces from a possibly less affluent family who make full use of the pram to transport the suitcases. They are returning home at the end of the Glasgow Fair. By the looks of it they enjoyed themselves. *(DW017)*

Some people always cut it fine. This dapper chap urges his family to get a move on as he lugs his golf clubs while pushing a pram laden down with the suitcases and other necessities for a fortnight away. *(DW018)*

Left: A fine view of a famous Glasgow landmark much used by holidaymakers bound for the coast. St Enoch Station closed in 1966 but the hotel soldiered on until '74, a monument to Victorian marble and mahogany. *(DW019)*

Below: The approaches to St Enoch Station in 1953 taken from the roof of another city landmark—Lewis's department store. The routes to the Clyde Coast and other Doon the Watter destinations curve off sharply to the right. Trains entering and leaving the station produced an intense squealing noise as the wheel flanges negotiated the curves. *(DW020)*

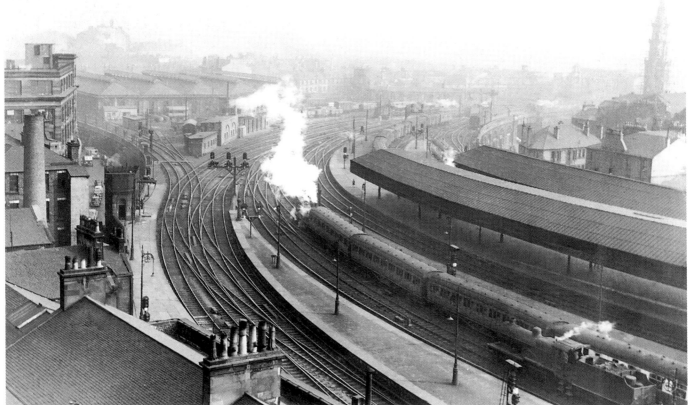

This is St Enoch Station on Easter Monday 1955 as day-trippers eagerly dash for a seat in a train to Saltcoats and Largs. The handsome locomotive shown was in its prime but ten years later it succumbed to the decline of steam and was scrapped at the shipbreakers at Faslane. On the left of the picture a sign proclaims Starlight Special which will evoke mixed memories for many West of Scotland people. The Starlights offered cheap, if not exactly direct, overnight travel to London. The lights suspended from the roof recall that in 1879 St Enoch was the first public area in Glasgow to be regularly lit by electricity. *(DW021)*

Left: Typical Fair holiday scene at Central Station in the 1950s. Crowds here are around platforms 1 and 2 and many of these people would be heading south of the border. The main platforms to the coast resorts, particularly Gourock, were on the far side of the station. *(DW022)*

Above: Two trainspotters put a station barrow to good use as they watch a departure from St Enoch. Locomotive number 40666 had Ardrossan as its home depot. Fair Saturday was a big day in the calendar for trainspotters since all the extra traffic attracted locomotives not normally seen in the city and there was much shuttling between Glasgow Central and St Enoch to maximise the number of new sightings! *(DW023)*

Some idea of the massive crowds that gathered at Glasgow's mainline terminals in the 1950s is conveyed by this scene taken outside Queen Street Station at the start of the Fair. Still plenty of servicemen in uniform around. Queen Street was the departure point for Helensburgh and Craigendoran, where steamers left mainly for the Argyllshire lochs but also for Cowal and beyond. *(DW024)*

Right: Passenger information announcement in the days before Tannoy! In dramatic style a railway official barks out the information through a megaphone in Queen Street Station in 1933. *(DW025)*

Craigendoran Pier was opened in 1883. The North British Railway ran steamers including the *Guy Mannering*, *Dandie Dinmont*, the *Gareloch* and briefly the *Meg Merrilies*. Later the *Jeanie Deans* was added to the fleet. Steamers from Craigendoran were often involved in races with the rival Caley steamers which left from Gourock. *(DW026)*

Right: At the height of their popularity, almost all the Clyde resorts boasted a classy swimming pool. This is Helensburgh's—not it has to be said, one of the most stylish—mobbed in the mid-1950s with youngsters cooling off watched by mums, dads, grannies and grandpas. *(DW028)*

Right: Who said the weather wasn't better in the good old days? The sun beats down on Helensburgh front in the 1950s. The shops are protected by the sun-shades of the era and the day-trippers in their deckchairs make the most of the warmth. *(DW027)*

Above: Yachting is a passion for many west coast Scots. Those who can afford it sail the Firth, those who can't watch from the many promenades. Yacht spotters old and new are highly knowledgeable about the comings and goings of famous craft. This spectacular action shot shows *Drum* in a stiff breeze. This 77ft yacht, once owned by pop star Simon le Bon, is now based at Rhu. Launched in 1985 it turned turtle when its keel snapped in that year's Fastnet race. The singer and other members of the crew were trapped and had to be rescued by a navy diver. *Drum* was repaired and went on to finish third in the Whitbread Round the World Race. Now it gets admiring glances on every appearance on the Firth. *(DW029)*

Above: This is the famous *Lucy Ashton* alongside the pier at Garelochhead. One of the most famous of the Clyde paddlers, the *Lucy* was built in Rutherglen in 1889 and gave 60 years' service. She had a distinctive red, white and black funnel and a stylish and spacious stern saloon. *(DW031)*

Below left: Blairvadach at Rhu was one of several Glasgow Corporation children's homes. Here in 1949 the children are graced with a visit from Lady McNeil and Mrs J Gardiner while the Matron, Miss Beverage, keeps a watchful eye on things. Clearly the fur coat was *de rigeuer* for visits in those days. *(DW030)*

Above: There is always something to see on a trip to the coast, and many journeys were made to catch sight of the mothballed fleet which lay in the Gareloch in the 1950s during the cold war. *(DW032)*

Above right: Loch Long, a fjord stretching northwards from Strone Point and Cove, was for almost 100 years frequented by pleasure steamers. The loch was a major communications route, not just for holidaymakers but for cargo and supplies of all sorts. Craigendoran was the starting point for most of the services and many ended at Arrochar. The *Marmion* is seen here at the pier probably before the start of the First World War. The famous Clyde paddler *Jeanie Deans* was also a regular visitor to the loch. *(DW033)*

Below right: The *Waverley*, seen at Arrochar Pier in July 1949, was a favourite on the Loch Goil and Arrochar run operating from Craigendoran. She became the property of the Paddle Steamer Preservation Society when she was sold by Caledonian MacBrayne for £1 after being withdrawn from service in the early 1970s. At the end of the millennium she still ventures to most of the Firth's resorts and round the Mull of Kintyre to the Inner Hebrides. *(DW034)*

Arrochar was a favourite stop on the highly-popular mystery tours on the buses which ran from Glasgow, often to the Argyllshire lochs. This picture captures a typical inter-war sunny day scene on the shores of Loch Long. Today Arrochar still attracts coachloads of tourists who enjoy the spectacular scenery of the lochs and glens—while trying to fend off the midges. *(DW035)*

At one stage there was great enthusiasm over hovercraft as a means of travel around the Clyde. Denny's of Dumbarton built this version which is shown at Finnart on Loch Long in 1965. Various services ran briefly but the noisy craft never really caught on. *(DW036)*

Inveraray on Loch Fyne was a stopping point for boats from Glasgow. Here, on a dreich day in the 1930s, a pipe band procession marches from the Inveraray Games park to meet the steamer. *(DW037)*

For landlubbers there is always something to watch on the Clyde—pleasure steamers, great liners, puffers and fishing boats. This group of holidaymakers at Rosneath pass a restful hour or two watching the dinghies skelp across the bay. *(DW038)*

Trips down the coast were, of course, seasonal and the pleasure vessels had the winter off, as it were. This Greenock streetscape is dominated by the *St Columba*, tied up waiting for spring, with shipyard cranes in the background. *(DW039)*

The current *Waverley*, still an eye-catcher in the 1990s, had a popular predecessor which was sunk at Dunkirk. Here the older *Waverley* is a tender to the liner *Transylvania* off Greenock. *(DW040)*

Above: Just downriver from Greenock, Gourock—with spectacular views of the Argyll hills—became a major terminus after being linked to Glasgow by rail. But it was also an important resort in its own right, particularly in the early days. This is the Gourock Highland Games in their heyday. *(DW041)*

Left: Most resorts boasted an annual festival, the centrepiece of which was the Gala Queen. This lucky lass is being crowned at Gourock by none other than famous American comedian Jack Benny in July 1952. Benny made a great play of theatrical meanness. On being presented with a beautiful cigar case to mark his visit to the Gala, he joked: 'But where are the cigars?' *(DW042)*

1938 at Gourock pier and the high fashion of the day included bunnets, trilbys and plus-fours, all in evidence among this group waiting to catch a ferry. *(DW043)*

This group of youngsters aren't going anywhere though. They are quite happy on the pier baiting their hooks and having a look over the *Gantock*, one of the Clyde's famous pilot boats. This picture was taken in 1957. At one time around 60 pilots were employed to guide ships around the 420 square miles of the river and its estuary. *(DW044)*

An aerial view of Gourock's harbour and the rail terminus. On the right is the famous Gourock seawater swimming pool, still functioning in the late 1990s, refurbished and heated. *(DW045)*

Camping holidays were very popular with many Clydesiders who couldn't afford the price of a B&B or who just preferred the freedom of a fortnight under canvas, miles from the tenements, shipyards and steelworks. This camp at Lunderston Bay south of Gourock was a Church of Scotland enterprise to provide holidays for the unemployed in the 1920s. *(DW046)*

DUNOON TO
WEMYSS BAY & ROTHESAY

It was not all fun and games on the Firth. The US Polaris nuclear missile submarines based at the Holy Loch were the focus for many demonstrations. Here in 1961 protesters take to the water in canoes to publicise their case. Polaris has gone now but the British Trident nuclear submarines still attract protests. *(DW047)*

In 1948 a young lady waits for assistance with her two trunks as she prepares to embark on the *St Columba* at Dunoon Pier, perhaps at the end of a two-week break in the resort. *(DW048)*

Right: For many people Dunoon is almost synonymous with the phrase 'Doon the Watter' and this 1954 photograph shows the *Queen Mary II*, one of the Clyde's most popular and best remembered pleasure craft, berthed at the pier. *(DW049)*

Left: A veritable armada of rowing boats crowd the Firth with the Cloch lighthouse in the background. The beach at Dunoon is equally busy with hardly an inch to spare. It's a case of deckchairs, deckchairs and more deckchairs. *(DW050)*

Above: A trip round the bay was a tradition. The board advertises a bargain voyage—adults one shilling, children sixpence—but this group seem happy enough with their books and newspapers. *(DW051)*

The autumn holidays down the Clyde could be very busy indeed. The original caption for this photograph says it was taken in the September holiday in 1956, described as Dunoon's busiest day of the year. In the background that Clyde favourite, the self-drive motorboat, putters along. *(DW052)*

Above: Fun for all the family. Here in the mid 1950s the family pooch, as ever, gets in on the action digging a hole in the sand—a favourite, if somewhat pointless, pastime for humans as well as canines. *(DW053)*

Right: These youngsters enjoying Dunoon indulge in the timeless pleasure of cracking open shells for precious bait. *(DW054)*

Left: This young fellow, complete with sou'wester and oilskins, looks as if he's dressed for a fishing excursion to the Grand Banks. But little John Henderson was just as pleased with his tiddlers as a Newfoundland fisherman would have been with giant cod. *(DW055)*

Above: Leaving the Dunoon foreshore for a row around the Firth, there is no problem in getting a shove-off from fellow holidaymakers always ready to join in the fun. *(DW056)*

An older and more elegantly posed group with a boatman. In the background a round the bay boat waits for its remaining seats to be filled. *(DW057)*

Right: The original caption describes this as a picture of Dunoon's "Lido". A lot less sophisticated than those found in continental resorts which, with the advent of the jet airliner, were eventually to take away much of the holiday traffic from these shores. But such primitive lidos—little more than rafts—still provided great enjoyment for the holidaymakers. Two of the most important lighthouses in the upper Firth are clearly visible—the Gantocks and the Cloch. *(DW058)*

Above: The Mediterranean resorts don't have a monopoly on the optional excursion to explore the delights of the surrounding area. This was always popular in Dunoon and these passengers are queuing up for day-trips to the pleasures of places like Inveraray Castle or Glendaruel. *(DW059)*

Right: Visitors from Moscow have their photograph taken at Dunoon. Another one for the family album, but not back in Russia. This cheery bunch had come all the way from Moscow, Ayrshire! *(DW060)*

Holiday snaps are vital for reliving the memories during the dark winter nights. The young chap in the centre is obviously delighted with his picture. In contrast the young lady standing on the left has a somewhat anxious air. *(DW061)*

57

The last Saturday in August is Cowal Games day, one of the most famous events on the circuit. This 1936 scene shows a crowd enjoying a leisurely afternoon on the slopes above the sports field. Despite the action there is always time to read a book or a programme. *(DW062)*

Right: This Cowal Games pole-vaulter manages to clear 11 foot 6 ¼ inches in 1933, some way below the current record of around 6 metres (almost 18 feet), but not bad considering the absence of modern facilities like foam rubber to soften the landing. The pioneers were a hardy breed. *(DW063)*

Highland dancing has always been one of the major attractions at the Cowal Games. These youngsters are competing in the under-sevens Highland Fling. *(DW064)*

Long before Hughie Green's *Opportunity Knocks* and the current rash of TV talent shows, the tradition of "Go-as-you-please" contests was well-established on the west coast of Scotland. Here Morna Archibald, an Edinburgh holidaymaker, takes the stage. Talent contests often featured in the variety shows run by entertainers like Archie McCulloch. *(DW065)*

Crowds throng Argyll Street, Dunoon. The La Scala cinema advertises *Toy Tiger* and *Break in the Circle,* starring Jeff Chandler and Forrest Tucker. For holidaymakers the cinema opened at 10.45am, ideal for a rainy day! Argyll Street was also at one time the home to another cinema called, rather unimaginatively but typically for the Clyde coast, The Picture House. *(DW066)*

Left: This panoramic view of Dunoon's west bay shows the long gardens stretching down to the shoreline. These gardens were very popular on warm days for sunbathing, tennis, cricket and other assorted pastimes. Lined up and ready for action are the boats for day-trips round the bay and rowing. In the distance is the coast road out towards Sandbank. *(DW067)*

Above: Speed and elegance combined as the *Lord of the Isles* sweeps up the Firth close inshore with the Cloch lighthouse in the background. This famous vessel sailed on the Glasgow to Inveraray run for around 20 years. Later she worked on other routes before finally being broken up in 1928. A namesake *Lord of the Isles* still graces the west coast, sailing for Caledonian MacBrayne. *(DW068)*

Left: As the great days of the Clyde steamers began to wane, a new class of smaller ship—the *Maids*—was introduced. Here the *Maid of Ashton*—echoes of a famous Clyde name—approaches Dunoon pier to berth forward of the *Cowal*. *(DW069)*

Below: Kirn on the Cowal peninsula with the ubiquitous *Waverley* tied alongside in 1953. *(DW070)*

Hunter's Quay is now better known as the Cowal terminus for Western Ferries' service from McInroy's Point just outside Gourock, but in its day it was an important stop on the Clyde pleasure steamer route. The *Caledonia* is seen berthing in 1948. Watching from the shore is a young woman wearing the latest high fashion—the much needed plastic mac! *(DW071)*

Left: A lasting memory of the Glasgow Fair—the trek down from the train to the pier at Wemyss Bay for the Rothesay ferry. Laughter and the expectation of a happy holiday with the passengers' footsteps echoing round the walkway. *(DW072)*

Above: The passengers emerged onto a spacious pier, dodging the cars waiting at Wemyss Bay to be loaded for Rothesay. This photograph was taken in 1959. *(DW073)*

An attractive picture that captures the atmosphere of the Fair holidays in the inter-war years. The paddle steamer *Glen Rosa* heels sharply as it makes a turn to port leaving Wemyss Bay bound for Rothesay. *(DW074)*

Passengers disembark after the crossing from Rothesay. The *Jupiter* dropped 1,100 passengers at Wemyss Bay on this trip at the end of the Glasgow Fair in 1956. The vessel in the background is the *Bute*. *(DW075)*

Passengers on board the steamer *Caledonia* en route to Rothesay enjoy some impromptu entertainment as a piper and Highland dancers, probably heading to the Highland Games, do a spot of rehearsal. *(DW076)*

The huge popularity of resorts like Rothesay, especially during the Fair, is captured in this picture of the sunny pier, packed as the *Duchess of Montrose* disembarks what are described in the original caption as "fair invaders", heading for their hotels and B&Bs. *(DW077)*

Left: The Clyde resorts produced a rich crop of characters over the years. This is Bob Buchanan who for more than 30 years played the fiddle on the pleasure boats from Rothesay during the season. *(DW078)*

Above: While some people took to caravans on their holidays, others preferred the cabin cruiser, like these berthed at Rothesay Harbour in July 1953. Much less sophisticated than the modern marina, but no doubt just as much fun. In the background is a good example of a ship's lifeboat converted to become a cabin cruiser, a common practice in those days. *(DW079)*

Left: The first task for any enterprising young schoolboy holidaymaker was to go to the tackle shop and purchase a fishing line, weights, hooks and bait. The next job was to find a suitable crack in the pier, or indeed to lean dangerously over the edge in search of the small fish that always swarmed around harbours. These youngsters were making the most of Rothesay pier. *(DW080)*

Above: A trip round the Bay. Here holidaymakers—complete with plastic macs, headscarves, and handbags grasped tightly—go down the slippery steps to take their places on the vessel. The skipper with flat cap watches them carefully while in the stern a gentlemen considers a soft hat ideal for such a jaunt. Perhaps one or two of the passengers might have enviously eyed the luxury cruiser tied up across the harbour. *(DW081)*

Endless fun was to be had on the various piers watching the fishermen mending their nets and landing their catches. For city folk the working practices of the seaside were fascinating. *(DW082)*

May 1955 and a somewhat top-heavy looking pleasure boat heads out for a trip up towards the Kyles of Bute. Toward Point is in the background and the passengers are in jolly mood waving to the photographer. *(DW083)*

This is the re-opening of perhaps Rothesay's most famous attraction, The Winter Gardens. The building had been allowed to decay but was re-opened in 1990 after an £850,000 restoration programme. Gracie Clark, one half of Clark and Murray, the celebrated variety act who played the venue many times, cut the ribbon. Sadly however, the project ran into financial difficulties in 1992 but now it looks like lottery money might save the day. Other regulars at The Winter Gardens included The Alexander Brothers and Mary Lee. Jack Anthony was another top-liner who first attracted attention at Rothesay. *(DW084)*

Above: Even in the "good old days" the Clyde coast seemed to get more than its fair share of rain, hence the shelters peppered around the proms at most of the resorts. This 1950 Rothesay group might have expected to be enjoying autumn sunshine but instead they had to make the most of dreich and depressing weather. *(DW085)*

Right: The famous Rothesay Entertainers could be relied on to brighten up a night out no matter the weather. This is the cast for season 1929. Impresarios Fyfe and Fyfe present Monty McVean, James Burns, Lewis Duckworth, Robert Fyfe, Billy Oswald, Sandy Conner, Phyllis Grey, Peggy Desmond, Lilly Anderson, Bond Rowel, Helen Hall, Clara Kenyon and Bijou Gordon. Performances were often twice a night and the Rothesay Entertainers launched many a star including the handsome young tenor from Motherwell, Robert Wilson, who became one of Scotland's top singers. Fyfe and Fyfe were also well-known to Glaswegians for running the "F and F" ballroom in Partick, now a bingo hall. *(DW086)*

FYFE & FYFE present the FAMOUS ROTHESAY (1929) ENTERTAINERS.

A visit to a Bute beach could involve a journey on the island's famous electric trams to Ettrick Bay. However, for hundreds the little beach at Rothesay itself was pleasure enough, especially if you liked company! *(DW087)*

Right: A spectacular view from Canada Hill behind Rothesay looking out over the bay and up to the Kyles of Bute. There is quite a lot of traffic in the bay—one steamer at the pier, another leaving while the Royal Yacht *Britannia* lies at anchor offshore. *(DW088)*

The Kyles of Bute is a magnificent, world-famous tourist attraction, spectacular from land and sea. On a calm and sunny day, a trip to remember. (DW089)

Below: Kames was a stopping point in the Kyles near Tighnabruaich. This photograph was taken in 1931. (DW090)

These happy holidaymakers enjoy a paddle as the *King Edward* makes a stop on a sail round the Kyles of Bute. The proximity of a waste pipe makes no difference for the indefatigable paddlers! *(DW091)*

In the days when TB and other respiratory diseases were commonplace, Glasgow Corporation used to send youngsters down the coast for fresh air and recuperation. One such destination was Caol Ruadh Residential School at Colintraive on the Kyles. The highlight for many youngsters was Wednesday and Saturday afternoons when they got their pocket-money and a teacher led an expedition from the house down to William McCreadie's shop. *(DW092)*

Caol Ruadh obviously didn't boast a heated swimming pool or indeed any of the fake palm trees or slides considered essential for a dip in the 1990s. Instead someone only had to say the word 'swim' and off they ran straight down into the Kyles. Despite all the apparent enjoyment, home sickness must have been something of a problem, because parents were allowed to visit only on certain dates—usually once every two months! *(DW093)*

LARGS to MILLPORT & ARRAN

Queen Mary II was a popular visitor to all the major Clyde resorts. Here we see her heading out from Tighnabruaich and the Kyles of Bute and on to the scenic Ayrshire coast for a new complement of passengers. The ship added *II* to her name in deference to Cunard's legendary *Queen Mary*. (DW094)

A paddler leaving Largs early in the century. The holidaymakers on shore and in the rowing boats are more formally dressed than people on holiday would be nowadays. But the lure of trying to row into the wake of a departing ship is still as strong. *(DW095)*

It's 1936 and Largs seafront is crowded with cars. Even more than 60 years ago the original caption talks about plans to beautify the area. There have been various schemes involving Largs seafront over the years and many changes, but cars and parking are still a problem. *(DW096)*

Above: The ubiquitous round the bay motor boat. This time the handsome looking *Daisy*, complete with flag and youngsters, is ready for an adventure out in the Firth. *(DW097)*

Left: At the end of a sail there was some hard work involved in bringing the boats ashore, but the holidaymakers, however young, were always ready to give the old salts a hand. *(DW098)*

Above: The holiday resorts provided fertile ground for that venerable institution, the seaside mission. This motorised preacher has musical backing in the form of a guitar and an accordion. His young "parishioners" on Largs foreshore in 1964 seem somewhat less than captivated. *(DW099)*

Right: Largs has devotees who regularly travel up from England to enjoy its delights. As in many other resorts, open air draughts games provided a source of relaxation. This Newcastle family work on a strategy. *(DW100)*

Model yachting can be a serious pastime. This is Saltcoats model yacht pond, described in the original caption as "one of the best in the west". The old salt is James Clunes with his model yacht, *Marilyn*. *(DW101)*

Right: Less sophisticated craft but no less fun for these boys. A trip to the boating pond was a must for the youngsters down the coast. These two are enjoying themselves at Largs in the 1950s. *(DW102)*

A snap to cherish in years to come. The beach photographer at Largs sets up a holiday picture for this typical family. In the background, a famous Largs landmark, Nardini's Cafe. Noticeably absent are the men of the family. Often the women and children went down to a Clyde resort for two weeks or a month with the man of the house joining as work permitted. *(DW103)*

Caravanning has always been a popular way to take advantage of the Clyde coast and its proximity to Glasgow and the heavily populated industrial neighbouring towns. This family, snapped just north of Largs, were using the 'van as a wind-break against the sea breezes to enjoy the sun to the full. *(DW104)*

The delightful little *Maid* ferries—which date from the 1950s—had their devoted followers. This was the *Maid of Cumbrae* on a breezy summer day in 1964. *(DW105)*

A spectacular view over Millport and Kames Bay capturing the dramatic beauty of the Firth of Clyde. Clouds dust Arran in the background. *(DW106)*

A journey on the Millport ferry is not normally reminiscent of rounding the Horn, but on this March day in '89, the *Isle of Cumbrae* took a battering on its way across the narrow channel between Largs and Cumbrae. The vessel is still in use and is often to be seen on the Portavadie-Tarbert route which links Cowal and Kintyre. *(DW107)*

Long before Elton John was in the charts with 'Crocodile Rock', these youngsters at Millport in the mid 1950s enjoyed clambering over what was sometimes also known as the 'Millport Monster'. Painted rocks were something of a feature on the Clyde coast: Millport also boasts Lion Rock and there were smaller examples dotted around the other resorts. *(DW108)*

Heading out west, on Cumbrae not California, and the background is Arran not the Rockies! With the advent of the jet and sunshine holidays, Clyde coast resorts tried all sorts of novelty events to retain the tourist trade. In the 1990s Millport launched an annual Country & Western festival in an effort to capitalise on the huge popularity of this kind of music in the West of Scotland. *(DW109)*

Left: This aerial picture of Ardrossan and Saltcoats beach captures the popularity of the area in 1966. The parked cars were photographed from the AA spotter plane, a feature of attempts to keep the traffic moving at the time. Now the job is done by helicopter. *(DW110)*

Above: At the peak of its popularity Saltcoats, like most resorts, boasted a lido complete with diving platforms and even small craft. Lined up in the background, an imposing row of elegant mansions. *(DW111)*

Left: For the newspaper photographer the Fair holiday was a time to follow the readers down to the coast. This view of the main shopping centre in Saltcoats on a Glasgow Fair Monday in July 1960 gives some idea of the buzz in a seaside town at the height of the holidays. *(DW112)*

Above: Festival time! Here the 1955 Saltcoats Queen of the Sea procession, headed by the town drummer and the Ardeer Cadet Pipe Band, make their way through the town to the crowning ceremony. A procession of floats follows the pipe band. *(DW113)*

Above: A nostalgic beach scene at Saltcoats. Deckchairs, sun-hats, ice-creams and prams are prominent and all sorts of ball games are under way on a hot summer's day in the fifties. *(DW114)*

Right & far right: Cafe society may be something of a modern phenomenon to Glasgow's yuppies, but to generations of day-trippers and holidaymakers Doon the Watter, a visit to the cafe was a big attraction. This is Settimo Cavani *(opposite page, left)* pictured outside the family cafe in Ardrossan around 1936. In 1989 *(right)* Mr Cavani shows off the photograph to a suitably impressed John and Jeannie Dunsmore from Rutherglen, who had been visiting the cafe for more than 50 years. *(DW115, DW116 opposite)*

Ardrossan, a busy port, was a starting-off point for sailings to the Isle of Man as well as Clyde coast destinations. The *Mona's Isle*, seen here departing in the 1960s, was a well-known name on this route. *(DW117)*

Above: Protection from the sun in the days before factor 50! A couple of towels sufficed as a barrier to sunburn, while the ubiquitous flask nestled in the shopping bag ready for a quick cuppa. The spade and pail and the beach ball were all at hand for later activity. This couple were all set to make the best of their day at the beach, if they could summon up the energy! *(DW118)*

Right: A vital part of a day out in the sun for the youngsters was a slug from a bottle of "ginger", in this case one of Garvie's legendary fruit crushes. The youngsters were on holiday from Camphill in Glasgow. *(DW119)*

The *Glen Sannox* was a well known name for a series of ferries on the Arran route. This early picture shows passengers disembarking at Whiting Bay by small boat from a steamer of that name. *(DW120)*

Up the coast from Whiting Bay lies Arran's main town, Brodick, which boasted this fine looking pier. The ship lying alongside is the *Duchess of Rothesay* of the Caledonian Steam Packet Company. This old paddler was a legend on the Arran run as well being used for excursions. During the First World War she towed a wrecked German Zeppelin to land after it had been captured in the North Sea. *(DW121)*

If you were lucky you might catch a glimpse of a liner doing her trials over the famous measured mile off Arran. Here in April 1936 the *Queen Mary* powers her way past the village of Sannox at the entrance to Glen Sannox. *(DW122)*

All good things had to come to an end and many youngsters shed a tear on the boat on the way home to Glasgow after a holiday in Arran. This boatload are leaving Lamlash in 1937. *(DW123)*

Right: Corrie on the road to Lochranza is another favourite Arran spot. On a sunny autumn day these youngsters are enjoying a spot of fishing. They're not after giant cod, but time spent at the end of the pier was often productive as well as enjoyable. *(DW124)*

Above: Country Post Offices, usually a focal point for the community, are always under threat and this one at Shiskine on the west coast of Arran overlooking the Kilbrannan Sound was no exception. In 1983 a local resident collects her pension while other villagers enjoy a cup of tea and a chat. Copies of the famous *Arran Banner* lie on the counter beside jars of traditional boiled sweets. *(DW125)*

Right: Some striking architectural imagination on view here as youngsters get down to the serious business of sandcastle building. Mind you, their dog looks less than impressed with this avant-garde creation. *(DW126)*

4

TROON TO AYR & KINTYRE

The Clyde's seafaring history is commemorated in the Scottish Maritime Museum in Irvine. That ubiquitous feature of the Clyde holiday the puffer is seen moored alongside a couple of lifeboats. The famous Clyde sailing ship *Carrick*, originally the *City of Adelaide*, and once a city centre sight at Glasgow's Clyde Street, is now being restored at Irvine. *(DW127)*

Irvine's Marymass Fair is one of the most important of the Ayrshire festivals. The coach driver in the foreground sports a shiny topper while in the background the riders of the sturdy Clydesdales are in less formal attire. The picture was taken in the High Street in 1952. *(DW128)*

A trip down the coast to watch the golf was always an attractive proposition. Back in 1972 there was a bit of glamour on view at Western Gailes, an all male club, which played host to the ladies' Curtis Cup in June of that year. Here legendary Scottish golfer, Belle Robertson (left) watches her American opponent, Laura Baugh, drive at the ninth. *(DW129)*

Naturists in Britain have never enjoyed the same level of tolerance as their counterparts abroad, particularly those in the Scandinavian countries. But in the late 1970s they were sanctioned to use a beach at Gailes, Irvine. The move proved to be controversial and eventually the naturists moved to other less prominent Scottish beaches. *(DW130)*

At Barassie, just round from Troon, everyone and their granny seems to have taken the car on to the beach and headed for a dip in 1967. *(DW131)*

Changed days. A mere 20 years later this warning sign was posted at Barassie. *(DW132)*

Keeping the hair dry was a top priority for young women when swimming even back in the early days. Plenty of smiles though, and in the background Troon beach looks busy. *(DW133)*

The train played a major role in opening up the Clyde resorts. This is Troon station looking towards Ayr. The locomotive was owned by the Glasgow and South Western Railway Company and the picture was probably taken before 1904. The footbridge was removed in 1985 as part of the electrification of the line. *(DW134)*

Troon town centre on a bright and blustery autumn day in the mid 1950s. The sunshine awnings are unrolled to protect the merchandise in the shop windows. *(DW135)*

Tog's Cafe is a Troon institution. As popular with the Sunday afternoon folk out for a run in the car as it is for the people who spend their fortnight's holiday in Troon. Here, in 1989, John Togneri is surrounded with the novelty goodies that have made his shop so popular with children of all ages. There is everything on display from rock false teeth to candy dummies! *(DW136, DW137 below)*

Troon is synonymous with golf and some of the greatest stars in the world have played there. Fifty years ago the crowds were following the great Max Faulkner who is seen over the right shoulder of Norman von Nida, in the beret, as they stroll towards the third green. The wisecracking Max is complete with plus-fours, collar and tie. *(DW138)*

Royal Troon frequently hosts the Open and always attracts huge crowds. In 1982 these somewhat untypical looking golf spectators found the weather warm enough to necessitate some cooling ice-cream. *(DW139)*

Prestwick airport came into its own during the Second World War, when it was a stopping-off point for war planes flying supplies from the factories of America to the battlefields of Europe. After the war commercial aviation steadily developed there. On a wet day in September 1946 a BOAC Constellation is unloaded. A visit to the airport viewing terrace was a real highlight for thousands of youngsters holidaying on the Ayrshire coast. *(DW140)*

A scene from the mid-thirties at Prestwick open air swimming pool, one of the most elegant and impressive on the Clyde coast. At the end of the day the pleasure of splashing around, slipping down the slide, or simply sitting in the sun watching the family have fun was probably much the same as at the more utilitarian pools of other resorts. *(DW141)*

Learning to swim was fun and important for safety at the seaside. There was nowhere better to do it than at one of the many pools where instructors were available to teach the youngsters. *(DW142)*

High diving was a great challenge. This 1930s shot shows an intrepid lady entertaining the crowds. Note boys in BB uniform in the extreme left beside the springboard. *(DW143)*

This young lad is happy with the challenge of coaxing his pony to maximum speed at Prestwick beach. *(DW144)*

Right: You didn't have to go on a gallop to enjoy the pony. This more sedate shot shows smaller children but a larger four-legged friend. *(DW145)*

What did you do when you got to the beach? Most important was to bury your brother or sister up to the neck in the sand. In this case, one-year-old Archie Kane was burying his cousin Tom at Ayr. *(DW146)*

Right: Golf, both professional and amateur, has always played a major role in Ayrshire life. This is July 1939, the Second World War is only a few months away but there's enjoyment and laughter on the Prestwick course as the famous Hector Thomson is stymied. Both he and his caddie study how to get his ball past the one on the lip of the hole. The crowd looks on hugely entertained. The stymie was a ploy made redundant by a later change of the rules. Again, the clothing on the golf course points to a different era. Thomson's opponent's caddie is replete with suit, collar and tie. *(DW148)*

Above: These days putting is usually a low-key fun affair with dad and the kids or even granny sauntering round the green sinking with ease putts that would make any seasoned pro tremble. But this game at Prestwick in 1922 was clearly a much more serious business. The gentleman on the left is carefully noting his score, the chap in the middle wears a hat, while the third member of the group, complete with bunnet, lines up a long putt. In the background are the bathing huts which were wheeled on to the beach to allow the modest to change before popping in to the briny for a paddle or a swim. *(DW147)*

Johnny Beattie was a great favourite at the Ayr Gaiety Theatre. Here he poses outside the theatre in July 1990 with the Jelly Rolls, a novelty song and dance act. They raise plenty of smiles from passers-by while enticing customers into the theatre. Others who played the Gaiety to great effect were Tom and Jack—The Alexander Brothers—and Jack Milroy and Mary Lee. Further up the coast at Largs, Barrfields Pavilion, now modernised, was another popular variety venue, where you could be entertained by the likes of Pat Kirkwood and Donald Peers. *(DW149)*

In the Mediterranean resorts Scots are famous for their rather reckless attitude to sunbathing. Back at home in the 1950s there was a much more cautious approach. Paper hats skilfully made out of newspapers, hankies tied over heads, sunglasses on every face. The gentleman on the right is lounging in his deckchair complete with his boots. A sight to remember! *(DW150)*

In the early 1930s style counted for a lot. A dip required the proper striped swimwear while a mere paddle meant that you didn't even have to take off your collar and tie. Lift up the skirts, take off the boots and in you went. *(DW151)*

132

Left: About twenty years later and this douce gentleman keeps up the well-dressed approach to paddling complete with hat and walking stick. *(DW152)*

Above: Another classic paddling shot as temperatures soar at Ayr in August 1955 and people of all ages, in all states of attire, take to the water. *(DW153)*

Left & above: The timeless attraction of the Punch and Judy would always draw a crowd on the beach, as these two pictures confirm. The 1930 version is on a pair of bicycle wheels, obviously the easier to move around. The stage looks slightly different in the fifties version but the characters are the same as is the attention they get from the youngsters. *(DW154, DW155 above)*

All sorts of showbusiness attractions, often sponsored by newspapers, went down the coast following the Fair crowds. Here the *Bulletin* newspaper and Mullard, who made radios, have given out balloons to youngsters. In the background the *Bulletin*, which was a picture paper published by the owners of the *Herald* and the *Evening Times*, has a board showing seaside scenes. This photograph was taken in the 1930s at Gourock. *(DW156)*

Right: A favourite ploy when on the beach was to build your own loch fed from the sea. Here in Ayr little Stewart Howieson, aged two, of Broxburn enjoyed the pool and his toy liner, not unlike the *Queen Elizabeth*. *(DW157)*

No fun to be had with the pail and spade today as the heavens opened and the rain pours down on Ayr promenade in 1977. These two youngsters are making the best of it, though. The beach huts were a feature of that era. *(DW158)*

Ayr harbour with its thriving fishing fleet was always an attraction, especially when the boats were landing their catch. This photograph was taken in 1968. *(DW159)*

Left: Again the fishing fleet is a feature in this aerial view of Ayr. The town's hotels and boarding houses still cater for the twin attractions of Burns country and beaches. *(DW160)*

Above: Burns's legacy is to be found all around Ayrshire. This public house in High Street, Ayr, sports the name Tam O'Shanter. The locals are enjoying a pint of beer while the barmaid points something out to them—perhaps it's "time to drink up, please". It's the 1950s when opening hours were less generous. *(DW161)*

Above: One of Ayr's biggest attractions is the racecourse. This is the finish of the 1984 Gold Cup. Able Albert (far left) sneaked up on the stand rail to pip No 15 Alakh in a memorable finish. *(DW163)*

Right: Two contrasting styles as these gents—one with the pinstriped trousers, coat and top hat, the other in less spectacular garb—watch the progress of a race in 1947. *(DW164)*

Left: A magnificent picture from 1931 capturing the essence of the time as the racing set with trilbys, flat caps, plus-fours and bowler hats watch the progress of a race through their binoculars, willing their horse to come through on the home straight. *(DW165)*

In the heyday of Clyde holidays, galas and festivals were great crowd-pullers for locals and visitors alike. This is Ayr Pageant in 1934. *(DW165)*

Butlin's Holiday Camps, established in the inter-war years, were extremely popular. This picture shows the opening of the camp at the Heads of Ayr by Mrs Tom Johnston, wife of the legendary Secretary of State for Scotland. Also in the picture is Sir Harry Lauder who is being welcomed by the man who started it all, Mr Billy Butlin. *(DW166)*

The chairlift, a major feature of the old Butlin's, was opened in 1959 at a cost of £30,000. The attraction was inaugurated by Eve Boswell, a South African singer who was a great favourite in Glasgow Alhambra's *Five Past Eight* shows. *(DW167)*

Below: Entertainment was a round the clock affair at Butlin's. There was no escape even at mealtimes. Here entertainers Tony Middleton and Chris Armstrong serenade the diners, one of whom looks particularly unimpressed! *(DW168)*

Glamour 1960s style, complete with scarves and rollers to complement the shorts. A bevy of young beauties head out for some Butlin's fun. The famous chalets are in the background. *(DW169)*

This scene outside Butlin's could be interpreted in several different ways. Clearly it was a much loved holiday camp but with an entrance sporting so many security signs, barriers and warnings, it wasn't immediately obvious that behind the facade lay a haven of pleasure for holidaymakers. *(DW170)*

Complete contrast to the hustle and bustle of Butlin's just down the coast is the attractive little fishing village of Dunure. Plenty to do here—scramble around the clifftops, picnic on a wide meadow above the village or wander down to the harbour and watch the fishermen. *(DW171)*

148

Culzean Castle is another major Ayrshire attraction, particularly popular for day visits. It was gifted to the National Trust in 1945 and the grounds subsequently became a country park. There are excellent picnic grounds, tree-lined walks and of course the impressive interior of the castle. Two of the castle's more recent claims to fame were the fact that U.S. President Dwight D Eisenhower had the National Guest Flat put at his disposal during his lifetime and at one point the castle was the home of comedian Jimmy Logan. *(DW172)*

Above: Turnberry Hotel is one of the most elegant on the Ayrshire coast. As such it was a fitting host for a Concours d'Elegance contest in 1959. The eye-catching car in the foreground is a Daimler convertible owned by Mrs G Dempsey. *(DW173)*

Right: Clyde holidaymakers were usually partial to a refreshment. This is the inside of Turnberry Hotel in the 1950s. The original caption says that this is the "super cocktail bar newly opened and reputed to be the most modern outside of Hollywood"! The barmen are at the ready but the drinkers are conspicuously absent. *(DW174)*

Above: When golf's Open Championship is played in places like Turnberry and Troon the golf stars often bring their families along with them to enjoy the Clyde coast. This could be any family mucking around in the golf course but the golfer on the right is Open winner and current TV golf pundit Johnnie Miller. His young son is playing with the daughters of Jack Nicklaus at Turnberry in '77. *(DW175)*

Left: These two youngsters enjoy the thrills of a merry-go-round. The six-year-old girl takes a bicycle ride while her three-year-old brother dreams of Grand Prix glory. *(DW176)*

151

The boating pond at Girvan was a favourite spot for children and also provided a quiet rest for the parents. This picture of a gala event was taken in 1938. *(DW177)*

A family enjoying a bracing run along Girvan sands. In the days of long hours in factories, yards or mines the seaside break was a real delight for families. *(DW178)*

One of Girvan's most famous characters was William Sloane (centre), known as the "Geisha". In this 1950s shot he had popped onto the fishing boat *Minicoy* in the harbour for a chat with Willie Marshall and Eric McIlwraith. *(DW179)*

Another old-timer, photographed at Girvan in the 1950s, was George Ingram who at 68 was the oldest member of the lifeboat crew—it is said that he had saved 22 non-swimmers from drowning. *(DW180)*

Right: An aerial view of the harbour at Girvan, towards the southern extremities of the Firth. *(DW181)*

On the other side of the Clyde estuary, on the Kintyre peninsula, the fishing port of Tarbert has always been a favourite holiday spot. As this 1983 picture shows it is also popular with yachtsmen. According to the caption there were 240 boats filling the harbour during the Tomatin Series. Who counted? *(DW182)*

Right: This most attractive little village, on the east coast of Kintyre, is Carradale. There are beautiful views across the Kilbrannan Sound to Arran and inland to the mountains. The new harbour was completed in 1959. The shore road wandering down through the centre of the picture is now edged with homes, many used by summer holidaymakers. Carradale and neighbouring Dippen and Waterfoot continue to be popular areas for summer homes for Glaswegians. *(DW183)*

Left: Carradale's older, elegant pier was a regular stop for the well-known stylish steamers *Dalriada* and *Davaar* which served Campbeltown and the Kintyre peninsula. The importance of the sea links can be gauged by the number of people on the pier. This was August of 1939. *(DW184)*

Above: Holidaymakers were always pleased to be entertained by the ship's band. Such bands were a great feature of many of the trips, especially longer ones like the Gourock to Campbeltown run. These particular entertainers were making a late 1940s journey all the more enjoyable. Requests were a speciality! *(DW185)*

Campbeltown is not exactly a beach resort but here in the 1960s this rather tiny sand trap was being made full use of by the holidaymakers. *(DW186)*

Campbeltown once boasted almost 40 distilleries. Scots entertainer Andy Stewart wished in song that Campbeltown loch could be whisky, and in fact at times so much distillery waste found its way into the water that it was said to almost smell of whisky. These intriguing model boats, in the form of a merry-go-round, were apparently the creation of a local cycle agent. *(DW187)*

Left: Many, many a child spent a day on a pier down the Clyde coast never noticing the yachts or pleasure steamers round about them. All attention was concentrated on getting a catch from the sometimes oily waters around a harbour. These youngsters were enjoying themselves at Campbeltown in 1960. *(DW188)*

Above: The Second World War disrupted many Clyde services so this was a memorable occasion in Campbeltown—1 June 1946, when the *Duchess of Hamilton* restarted service after a gap of nearly seven years. *(DW189)*

Left: A post-war shot of Campbeltown from the air showing the old and the new pier, the small beach on the left and the striking island of Davaar linked to the mainland at low-tide by a pebble bar. The town itself was founded under James VI's policy of establishing settlements in distant parts of the country to encourage trade. At the height of the distilling boom the town was often said to be engulfed in a fog of peat smoke. The mansions of the distillery owners still line the northern shore of the loch. *(DW190)*

Above: A famous trip was from Glasgow by train and boat to Campbeltown and then across the narrow Mull of Kintyre to the Atlantic to play golf at Machrihanish or simply admire the huge rollers coming in after a long uninterrupted run across the ocean. In the early days visitors used Kintyre's only railway which ran between Machrihanish and Campbeltown. The railway had been built before the turn of the century to serve the Machrihanish colliery, but also provided a popular passenger link. The service ceased in 1932. The huge seas which crash on the beach are now a magnet for canoe and surfboard enthusiasts. A long journey that started at the Broomielaw has ended with the thunder of the Atlantic rollers on one of Scotland's finest beaches. *(DW191)*

Sailing into history. The great days of the Clyde steamers are over. Paddlers no longer race from Gourock and Craigendoran to Kilcreggan. No more do dozens of ships criss-cross the Firth, their decks and saloons packed with happy holidaymakers. The ships' bands have fallen silent. The car has largely taken over from bus and train. But the magic of the Firth of Clyde is enduring and once-bustling resorts renew themselves for a different style of tourism. In the new millennium the Clyde Coast will continue to attract and refresh visitors, not just from industrial Scotland, but from around the world. *(DW192)*